Stories for a Grad's Heart

Stories
for a Grad's
Heart

COMPILED *by* ALICE GRAY

MULTNOMAH PUBLISHERS · SISTERS, OREGON

STORIES FOR A GRAD'S HEART
published by Multnomah Publishers, Inc.

© 2001 by Multnomah Publishers, Inc.
International Standard Book Number: 1-57673-776-4

Cover inset photo by SuperStock
Cover background photo by Photodisc
Design by The Office of Bill Chiaravalle | www.officeofbc.com

Scripture quotes are taken from:
The Holy Bible, New International Version (NIV)
© 1973, 1984 by International Bible Society,
used by permission of Zondervan Publishing House

Holy Bible, New Living Translation (NLT)
© 1996. Used by permission of Tyndale House Publishers, Inc. All rights reserved.

The Message, © 1993 by Eugene H. Peterson

The Holy Bible, New King James Version (NKJV). © 1984 by Thomas Nelson, Inc.

Multnomah is a trademark of Multnomah Publishers, Inc.,
and is registered in the U.S. Patent and Trademark Office.
The colophon is a trademark of Multnomah Publishers, Inc.

Printed in China

For information:
MULTNOMAH PUBLISHERS, INC. • POST OFFICE BOX 1720 • SISTERS, OREGON 97759

03 04 05 06 07 08—10 9 8 7 6 5 4 3 2 1

Tomorrow's Dreams

When you have tomorrow in your heart
you never run out of dreaming room.
And dreaming is the stuff of hope.

JEAN PIERRE GODET

CONTENTS

CONTENTS

Remembering

by MAX LUCADO

from THE INSPIRATIONAL STUDY BIBLE

If you've ever been part of the following scenes, you'll never forget it.

Inside the house is a quiet bedroom. Last spring's prom photo sits on the bedside table. A dried homecoming mum hangs from the bulletin board. Outside the house is a packed car. Both trunk and seat are full of clothes, books, and stereo. What was in the room is now in the car. The one who used to live in the room is about to drive the car...to college.

Both parent and child are stunned by the moment. What happened to childhood? Who fast-forwarded the years? Why, just yesterday this child was filling the house with cartwheels and play dough—now look. He's so tall. She's such a beauty. The child is grown.

The grown child is equally stunned. The road ahead looks lonely and long. There is safety in these walls. Protection. Security. Those pleas for independence so recently voiced are unheard today. "Just say the word, Dad, I'll stay. Just ask me, Mom, I won't leave."

But Mom and Dad know better. They know that love releases the loved. They know the training is over. The last bell has rung. The class is dismissed, and the application has begun.

And so parents and child hesitate at the side of the car. There's no time to teach new truths. There's no time to instill values or lay foundations. There is only one word that can be said—*remember.* Remember who loves you. Remember what matters. Remember what is right and what is wrong.

Remember.

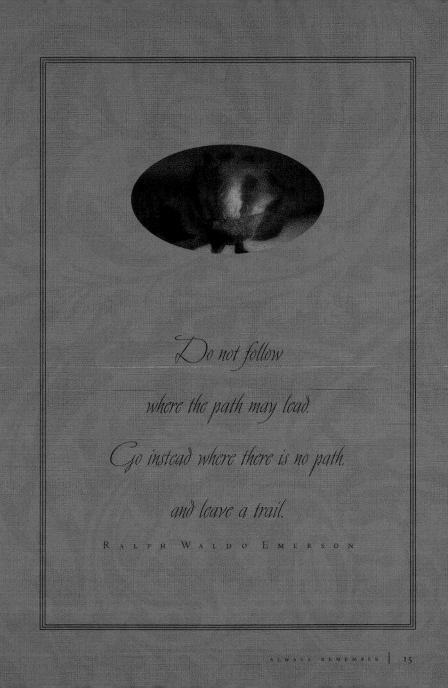

Do not follow

where the path may lead.

Go instead where there is no path,

and leave a trail.

RALPH WALDO EMERSON

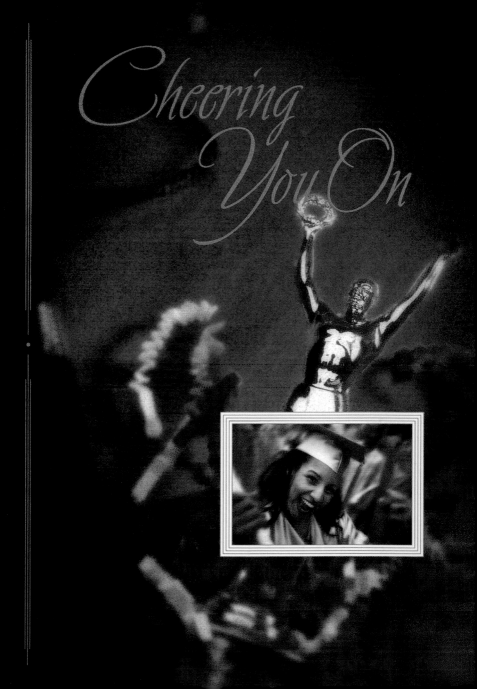

Cheering You On

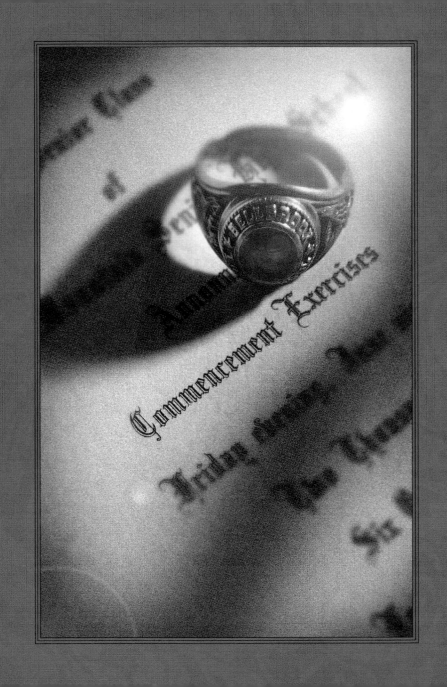

GRADUATION SPEECH

by TIM WILDMON

retold by ALICE GRAY

Ninety-three students marched into the crowded auditorium to the sleepy notes of *Pomp and Circumstance*. Their maroon caps and gowns made them look almost as grown-up as they felt. Dads swallowed hard behind proud smiles, and moms brushed away tears.

There would be no prayer at this ceremony: no invocation, no blessing, no closing benediction. This wasn't by the students' choice. A recent court ruling had prohibited it.

The principal and all the students who spoke were careful to stay within the guidelines allowed by the ruling. They gave inspiring speeches, but no one mentioned divine guidance or asked for blessings on the graduates or their families. The speeches were nice—challenging, even—but they were fairly routine.

Until the final speech.

A student strode to the microphone and stood silently for a

moment. Then he delivered the entire content of his speech—a resounding sneeze. On cue, the rest of the students rose to their feet, and in unison said, "God bless you." The audience exploded in applause.

This graduating class found a unique way to invoke God's blessings on their future—with or without the court's approval.

To move the world,

we must first move ourselves.

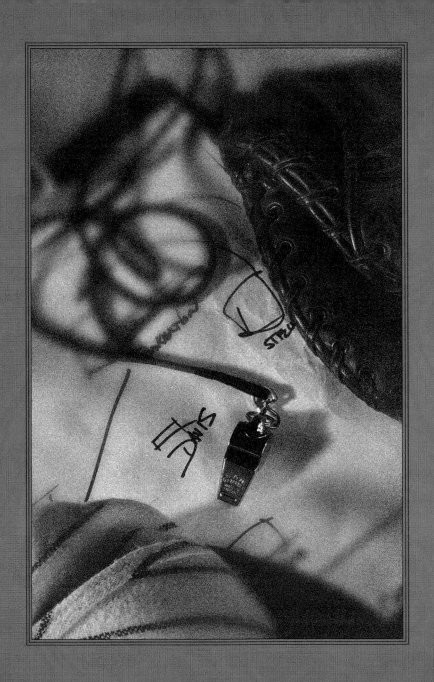

You Can Do It

by RICKY BYRDSONG

with DAVE and NETA JACKSON
from COACHING YOUR KIDS IN THE GAME OF LIFE

I remember it like it was yesterday. Tenth grade, Frederick Douglass High School in Atlanta. Tall and gangly, I was pushing my way through the crowded hallway. All of a sudden a big, booming voice pealed like a thunderclap behind me, "Hey, son!"

It was Coach William Lester. He was a big, barrel-chested man, six feet, four inches. Besides being the junior varsity basketball coach, he also had a reputation as the school disciplinarian, so the first thing I thought was, Uh-oh, somebody's in trouble. He fixed me with his piercing eyes and bellowed, "Yeah, you, son!"

Weak-kneed, I started walking toward him. Oh, my, what had I done? I stopped in front of him, all six feet, five inches of me trembling in my shoes.

"Son!" he said, looking me up and down. "You're too big to be walking these halls and not playing basketball. I'll see you in the gym at 3:30—today."

"But Coach!" I sputtered. "I've never played basketball. I don't have any basketball clothes or shoes."

"Son! Did you hear what I said? I'll see you at 3:30!" And he walked away.

So I went.

And from that day until now, there's no question in my mind that everything that has happened to me since—becoming a basketball player, then a coach, raising my three kids, writing a book—is a result of that day when coach called me out and said, "Hey, son! Yes, you!"

Up until that point, I hadn't been a troublemaker, but I was drifting. I had no idea what my goals were or where I was heading.

My mom, like so many parents—especially single, working parents—really didn't have time to think about those things. Her goals were pretty basic. "I don't want Ricky on drugs. I don't want him running with the wrong crowd."

Coach Lester helped me see something bigger out there. I remember when he told me, "You can get a college scholarship."

When I said, "But I don't know how. I don't have it." He said, "Yes, you do. I'm going to show you. I'm going to work with you. You can do it."

And he was right. I knew it the day I set foot on a college campus, scholarship in hand. He believed in me. I couldn't let him down.

Many times since the day I heard that big voice bellow, "Hey, son!" I've thought: If only every kid had a Coach William Lester to believe in him, what a difference it would make.

Wanted

AUTHOR UNKNOWN

More to improve and fewer to disapprove.
More doers and fewer talkers.

More to say it can be done
And fewer to say it's impossible.

More to inspire others
And fewer to throw cold water on them.

More to get into the thick of things
And fewer to sit on the sidelines.

More to point out what's right
And fewer to show what's wrong.

More to light a candle
And fewer to curse the darkness.

It is my prayer for you, my fellow students,

that you will actively seek out opportunities

to dole out encouragement as though it were breath

mints at a garlic and Limburger cheese festival.

ADAM BOLLEN
GRADUATION SPEECH

KEEPER OF THE SPRING

by CHARLES R. SWINDOLL

from IMPROVING YOUR SERVE

The late Peter Marshall, an eloquent speaker and for several years the chaplain of the United States Senate, used to love to tell the story of "The Keeper of the Spring," a quiet forest dweller who lived high above an Austrian village along the eastern slopes of the Alps. The old gentleman had been hired many years ago by a young town council to clear away the debris from the pools of water up in the mountain crevices that fed the lovely spring flowing through their town. With faithful, silent regularity, he patrolled the hills, removed the leaves and branches, and wiped away the silt that would otherwise choke and contaminate the fresh flow of water. By and by, the village became a popular attraction for vacationers. Graceful swans floated along the crystal clear spring, the millwheels of various businesses located near the water turned day and night, farmlands were naturally irrigated, and the view from restaurants was picturesque beyond description.

Years passed. One evening the town council met for its semi-annual meeting. As they reviewed the budget, one man's eye caught the salary figure being paid the obscure keeper of the spring. Said the keeper of the purse, "Who is the old man? Why do we keep him on year after year? No one ever sees him. For all we know the strange ranger of the hills is doing us no good. He isn't necessary any longer!" By a unanimous vote, they dispensed with the old man's services.

For several weeks nothing changed. By early autumn the trees began to shed their leaves. Small branches snapped off and fell into the pools, hindering the rushing flow of sparkling water. One afternoon someone noticed a slight yellowish brown tint in the spring. A couple days later the water was much darker. Within another week, a slimy film covered sections of the water along the banks and a foul odor was soon detected. The millwheels moved slower; some finally ground to a halt. Swans left as did the tourists. Clammy fingers of disease and sickness reached deeply into the village.

Quickly, the embarrassed council called a special meeting. Realizing their gross error in judgment, they hired back the old keeper of the spring…and within a few weeks the veritable river of life began to clear up. The wheels started to turn, and new life returned to the hamlet in the Alps once again.

Fanciful though it may be, the story is more than an idle tale. It carries with it a vivid, relevant analogy directly related to the times in which we live. What the keeper of the spring meant to the village, Christian servants mean to our world. The preserving, taste-giving bite of salt mixed with the illuminating, hope-giving ray of light may seem feeble and needless...but God help any society that attempts to exist without them! You see, the village without the Keeper of the Spring is a perfect representation of the world system without salt and light.

The only true happiness comes from

squandering ourselves for a purpose.

WILLIAM COWPER

THE BEST...NOT THE WORST

by TED ENGSTROM

*Y*ears ago, a group of brilliant young men at the University of Wisconsin seemed to have amazing, creative literary talent. They were would-be poets, novelists, and essayists. They were extraordinary in their ability to put the English language to its best use. These promising young men met regularly to read and critique each other's work. And critique it they did!

These men were merciless with one another. They dissected the most minute literary expression into a hundred pieces. They were heartless, tough, even mean in their criticism. The session involved such arenas of literary criticism that the members of this exclusive club called themselves the "Stranglers."

Not to be outdone, the women of literary talent in the university were determined to start a club of their own, one comparable to the Stranglers. They called themselves the "Wranglers." They too read their works to one another. But there was one great difference. The criticism was much softer, more positive, more encouraging. Sometimes, there was almost no criticism at all. Every effort, even the most feeble, was encouraged.

Twenty years later, when an alumnus of the university conducted an exhaustive study of his classmates' careers, he noticed a vast difference in the literary accomplishments of the Stranglers as opposed to the Wranglers. Of all the bright young men in the Stranglers, not one had made a significant literary accomplishment of any kind. From the Wranglers had come six or more successful writers, some of national renown, such as Marjorie Kinnan Rawlings, who wrote *The Yearling*.

Talent between the two? Probably the same. Level of education? Not much difference. But the Stranglers strangled, while the Wranglers were determined to give each other a life. The Stranglers promoted an atmosphere of contention and self-doubt. The Wranglers highlighted the best, not the worst.

So encourage each other

and build each other up,

just as you are already doing.

1 THESSALONIANS 5:11

NEW LIVING TRANSLATION

He who has a "why" to live for

can bear almost any "how."

Along the Path

AUTHOR UNKNOWN

water bearer in India had two large pots, each hung on an end of a pole, which he carried across his neck. One of the pots had a crack in it, and while the other pot was perfect and always delivered a full portion of water at the end of the long walk from the stream to the master's house, the cracked pot arrived only half full.

For a full two years, this went on daily, with the bearer delivering only one and a half pots full of water to his master's house. Of course, the perfect pot was proud of its accomplishments...perfect to the end for which it was made. But the poor cracked pot was ashamed of its own imperfection and miserable that it was able to accomplish only half of what it had been made to do.

After two years of what it perceived to be a bitter failure, it spoke to the water bearer one day by the stream. "I am ashamed of myself, and I want to apologize to you."

"Why?" asked the bearer. "What are you ashamed of?"

"I have been able, for these past two years, to deliver only half my load because this crack in my side causes water to leak out all the way back to your master's house. Because of my flaws, you have to do all of this work, and you don't get full value from your efforts," the pot said.

The water bearer felt sorry for the old cracked pot, and in his compassion he said, "As we return to the master's house, I want you to notice the beautiful flowers along the path."

Indeed, as they went up the hill, the old cracked pot took notice of the sun warming the beautiful wildflowers on the side of the path, and this cheered it some. But at the end of the trail, it still felt bad because it had leaked out half its load, and so again, the pot apologized to the bearer for its failure.

The bearer said to the pot, "Did you notice that there were flowers only on your side of the path, but not on the other pot's side? That's because I have always known about your flaw, and I took advantage of it. I planted flower seeds on your side of the path, and every day while we walk back from the stream, you've watered them. For two years I have been able to pick these beautiful flowers to decorate my master's table. Without you being just the way you are, he would not have had this beauty to grace his house."

Each of us has our own unique flaws. But if we will

allow it, the Lord will use our flaws to grace His Father's table. In God's great economy, nothing goes to waste. Don't be afraid of your flaws. Acknowledge them, and you too can be the cause of beauty. Know that in our weakness we find our strength.

I Wish for You

J A M E S   N .   W A T K I N S

I wish you truth for your decisions,

I wish you doubts to make you sure.

I wish you fear to give you caution,

I wish you courage to keep you pure.

But beyond these hopes and wishes,

One prayer soars high above.

I wish for you, my graduate—

Faith and hope and love.

I wish defeats to make you humble,

I wish success to let you soar.

I wish you tears to make you tender,

I wish you joy and so much more.

For beyond these hopes and wishes,

One prayer soars high above.

I wish for you, my graduate—

Faith and hope and love.

So as you stand and face tomorrow,

When life gets rough and tough.

There's someone who believes in you

With faith and hope and love.

So I wish for you, my graduate—

Faith and hope and love.

Fulfilling Your Dreams

Dreams are reached by

facing obstacles and climbing hills.

SARAH McGHEHEY

GRADUATION SPEECH

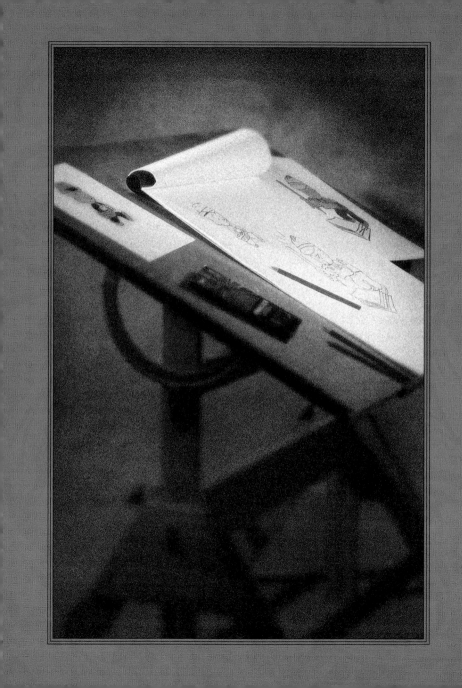

SPARKY

by EARL NIGHTINGALE

from MORE OF...THE BEST OF BITS AND PIECES

For Sparky, school was all but impossible. He failed every subject in the eighth grade. He flunked physics in high school, getting a grade of zero.

Sparky also flunked Latin, algebra, and English. He didn't do much better in sports. Although he did manage to make the school's golf team, he promptly lost the only important match of the season. There was a consolation match; he lost that, too.

Throughout his youth, Sparky was awkward socially. He was not actually disliked by the other students; no one cared that much. He was astonished if a classmate ever said hello to him outside of school hours.

There's no way to tell how he might have done at dating. Sparky never once asked a girl to go out in high school. He was too afraid of being turned down.

Sparky was a loser. He, his classmates...everyone knew it. So he rolled with it. Sparky had made up his mind early in life that if things were meant to work out, they would. Otherwise he would content himself with what appeared to be his inevitable mediocrity.

However, one thing was important to Sparky—drawing. He was proud of his artwork. Of course, no one else appreciated it. In his senior year of high school, he submitted some cartoons to the editors of the yearbook. The cartoons were turned down. Despite this particular rejection, Sparky was so convinced of his ability that he decided to become a professional artist.

After completing high school, he wrote a letter to Walt Disney Studios. He was told to send some samples of his artwork, and the subject for a cartoon was suggested. Sparky drew the proposed cartoon. He spent a great deal of time on it and on all the other drawings he submitted. Finally, the reply came from Disney Studios. He had been rejected once again. *Another loss for the loser.*

So Sparky decided to write his own autobiography in cartoons. He described his childhood self—a little boy loser and chronic underachiever. The cartoon character would soon become famous worldwide.

For Sparky, the boy who had such a lack of success in school and whose work was rejected again and again, was Charles Schulz. He created the "Peanuts" comic strip and the little cartoon character whose kite would never fly and who never succeeded in kicking a football—Charlie Brown.

Go confidently

in the direction

of your dreams.

HENRY DAVID THOREAU

CATSUP SOUP

by CYNTHIA HAMOND

A tribute to GREG WOZNICK from his daughters

My father learned how to make catsup soup in college. He didn't major in culinary arts; he just learned which waitresses in which restaurants would give him a free cup of hot water and then look the other way while he stirred in their catsup to make his supper.

He was the youngest of nine children from a North Dakota prairie town. When he went to college, he found many people willing to teach him a lesson or two.

Some tried to teach him that he wasn't a first-generation American whose family left everything and fled to our country seeking freedom. No, he was just another one of those immigrants.

Others decided that his accent didn't mean that he was probably bilingual, it just meant that he was ignorant.

Working five jobs to pay his way through college and sleeping in someone's car when he couldn't afford room and board didn't make him determined, it only made him the poor son of a coal miner.

But my father never learned these lessons. He never learned them because he just didn't hear them.

His inner voice was louder than their words.

His dreams were so real that to live them was worth the price he paid.

His vision was up and over those who would try to keep him down.

My father learned the lessons for his lifetime.

The same lessons he passed on to his students when he had achieved what he set out to do.

To be a teacher.

And teach he did. In the classroom and on the basketball court. His children and then his grandchildren. Executives, CEOs, and convention rooms filled with hundreds of people.

He taught what he himself had lived.

That your dreams must come from your heart's deepest desires. Only then will the barriers come down before you.

To know your heart, you must know yourself.

You are who you decide to be, not who other people decide for you.

You were created and intended for greatness.

Be noble. Stand the higher ground.

He taught them to see their possibilities.

And he taught them to see the soup in a hot cup of water
and a bottle of catsup.

Live!

FROM GRADUATION SPEECH

Live!
Love and cherish life.
Make friends, memories, and plans.
Your life is about you, but life is not about you.
Fall in love.
Love the fall and winter and spring and summer.
Ski, skate, sing, and dance.
Smell the rain and the chocolate chip cookies.
Take all the time you need, but don't waste it.
Catch the big one with your dad.
Go on that trip with your mom.
Love children, for you were once one.
Learn from your elders, and one day you'll have their wisdom.
Seek the truth. Find it in yourself, others, and the God of your faith.
Be patient and gentle.
Most of all, truly live.

If the Dream Is Big Enough...

by Cynthia Stewart-Copier

I used to watch her from my kitchen window and laugh. She seemed so small as she muscled her way through the crowd of boys on the playground. The school was across the street from our home and I would often stand at my window, hands buried in dishwater or cookie dough, watching the kids as they played during recess. A sea of children, and, yet to me, she stood out from them all.

I remember the first day I saw her playing basketball. I watched in wonder as she ran circles around the other kids. She managed to shoot jump shots just over their heads and into the net. The boys always tried to stop her but no one could.

I began to notice her at other times, on that same blacktop, basketball in hand, playing alone. She would practice dribbling and shooting over and over again, sometimes until dark.

One day I asked her why she practiced so much. As she turned her head, her dark ponytail whipped quickly around and she looked directly in my eyes. Without a moment of hesitation she said, "I want to go to college. My dad wasn't able to go to college, and he has talked to me about going for as long as I can remember. The only way I can go is if I get a scholarship. I like basketball. I decided that if I were good enough, I would get a scholarship. I am going to play college basketball. I want to be the best. My daddy told me if the dream is big enough, the facts don't count." Then she smiled and ran toward the court to recap the routine I had seen over and over again.

Well, I had to give it to her—she was determined. I watched her through those junior high years and into high school. Every week, she led her varsity team to victory. It was always a thrill to watch her play.

One day in her junior year, I saw her sitting in the grass, head cradled in her arms. I walked across the street and sat down in the cool grass beside her. Quietly I asked what was wrong. "Oh, nothing," came a soft reply. "I am just too short." The coach told her that at five-foot-five she would probably never get to play for a top-ranked team—much less be offered a scholarship—so she should stop dreaming about college.

She was heartbroken and I felt my own throat tighten as I sensed her disappointment. I asked her if she had talked to her dad about it yet.

She lifted her head from her hands and told me that her father said those coaches were wrong. They just did not understand the power of a dream. He told her that if she really wanted to play for a good college, if she truly wanted a scholarship, that nothing could stop her except one thing—her own attitude. He told her again, "If the dream is big enough, the facts don't count."

The next year, as she and her team went to the Northern California Championship game, she was seen by a college recruiter who was there looking at the opposing team. She was indeed offered a scholarship, a full ride, to a Division I, NCAA women's basketball team. She accepted. She was going to get the college education that she had dreamed of and worked toward for all those years. And that little girl had more playing time as a freshman and sophomore than any other woman did in the history of that university.

Late one night, during her junior year of college, her father called. "I'm sick, honey. I have cancer. No, don't quit school and come home. Everything will be okay. I love you."

He died six weeks later—her hero, her dad. She did leave school those last few days to support her mother and care for her father. Late one night, during those final hours before his death, he called for her in the darkness.

As she came to his side, he reached for her hand and struggled to speak. "Rachel, keep dreaming. Don't let your dream die with me. Promise me," he pleaded. "Promise me."

In those last few precious moments together she replied, "I promise, Daddy."

Those years to follow were hard on her. She was torn between school and her family, knowing her mother was left alone with a new baby and three other children to raise. The grief she felt over the loss of her father was always there, hidden in that place she kept inside, waiting to raise its head at some unsuspecting moment and drop her again to her knees.

Everything seemed harder. She struggled daily with fear, doubt, and frustration. A severe learning disability had forced her to go to school year-round for three years just to keep up with requirements. The testing facility on campus couldn't believe she had made it through even one semester. Every time she wanted to quit, she remembered her father's words, "Rachel, keep dreaming. Don't let your dream die. If the dream is big enough, you can do anything! I believe in you." And of course, she would remember the promise she made to him.

My daughter kept her promise and completed her degree. It took her six years, but she did not give up. She can still be found sometimes as the sun is setting, bouncing a basketball. And often I hear her tell others, "If the dream is big enough, the facts don't count."

Obstacles are those frightful things you see

when you take your eyes off the goal.

HANNAH MORE

Yesterday and Tomorrow

ROBERT J. BURDETTE

There are two days in every week about which we should not worry—two days that should be kept free from any fear and apprehension. One of these days is Yesterday, with its mistakes and cares, its aches and pains, its faults and blunders. Yesterday has passed forever beyond our control. All the money in the world cannot bring back Yesterday. We cannot undo a single act we performed; we cannot erase a single word we said; we cannot rectify a single mistake. Yesterday has passed forever beyond recall. Let it go.

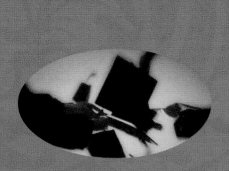

The other day we should not worry about is Tomorrow, with its possible adversities, its burdens, its large promise and poor performance. Tomorrow also is beyond our immediate control. Tomorrow's sun will rise either in splendor or behind a mass of clouds—but it will rise. And until it does, we have no stake in Tomorrow, because it is as yet unborn.

That leaves us but one day—Today! And a person can fight the battles of just one day.

Yesterday and Tomorrow are futile worries. Let us, therefore, resolve to journey no more than one day at a time.

ROSY'S MIRACLE

by NANCY JO SULLIVAN

from MOMENTS OF GRACE

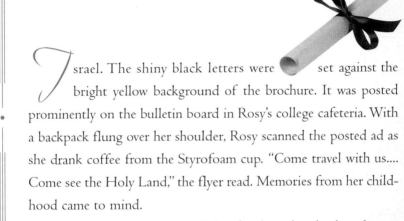

*srael. The shiny black letters were set against the bright yellow background of the brochure. It was posted prominently on the bulletin board in Rosy's college cafeteria. With a backpack flung over her shoulder, Rosy scanned the posted ad as she drank coffee from the Styrofoam cup. "Come travel with us.... Come see the Holy Land," the flyer read. Memories from her childhood came to mind.

She remembered sitting with her family at church when she was ten years old, the pastor showing slides of Israel. Enchanted, she memorized each sacred place: the rough terrain of the Jordan River, the aqua blue of the Mediterranean Sea, the white stones that framed the tomb of Jesus.

"Please, Lord...let me see Israel someday," she had prayed.

The memory quickly faded as the bell for her next class rang. Jotting down the phone number on the brochure, she rushed off to a lecture.

Later that night in her dorm room as she was unable to concentrate on her studies, she held the phone number in her hand. She wanted to call but she knew an international trip was not in her budget. Finances were tight in her family. She was working her way through school, subsidizing financial aid with a meager waitress salary.

She picked up the phone anyway. "It won't hurt to call," she told herself.

A youth pastor answered. He was happy to share the Israel itinerary.

"How much will the trip cost?" she asked.

"A thousand dollars," the pastor replied.

"I'm sorry," she said. "I can't afford it."

"I won't be needing payment until July 1. That will give you three months," he said kindly.

The pastor seemed to sense her disappointment. "Maybe God wants to work a miracle for you. Why don't you pray about it?" he said.

"A miracle," Rosy muttered as she hung up the phone.

She had never thought of asking God for something as big as a miracle.

Her daily prayers had always been generic: "Lord, bless my family...protect my friends...help me with this exam..."

How could she ask God for a thousand dollars? God needed to tend to those whose needs were greater than hers—the poor, the lonely, the starving of the world.

She crumpled the phone number and threw it in the wastebasket.

For hours she tried to distract herself with homework, but she kept hearing the pastor's words: *Why don't you pray about it?*

Soon she was on her knees, her head bowed, her hands folded: "Lord, I'm sorry for asking for so much. I know you are busy answering more urgent prayers," she began, "but I'd like to go to Israel."

As the weeks passed, Rosy prayed every night that God would provide a way for her to finance the trip. Though her intercessions were heartfelt, she always apologized for her request.

"Lord, I know this is a lot to ask," she would pray.

The first day of July arrived. Rosy woke up early just as the sun was rising. She was staying at a girlfriend's house in a private room decorated with white linens and a silver wall cross.

Rosy lingered in bed for a while. "It's the last day to turn in the money," she told herself.

A Bible lay close by at her bedside. She opened it and began reading a passage from the book of Ezekiel: "I am going to send you to the nation of Israel," the verse proclaimed.

Could the words be meant for her? Rosy closed her eyes. "Lord, give me faith to believe that You can still work a miracle."

Minutes later, her friend knocked on the door. "Let's go out to breakfast," she suggested.

As the two of them drove to a restaurant, her friend pulled into the driveway of a steepled church. "I'll be right back; I've got to drop something off," she told Rosy.

As Rosy waited in the car, she looked toward the garage of the church rectory. Inside, she saw a tall man in a flannel shirt. He was fixing a bicycle. She recognized him. He had often ridden past her college, and they had waved to each other many times.

Leaving the car, she walked toward the garage and exchanged small talk with the man. His name was Lenny, and he was a seminarian. He wanted to be a pastor and was living at the church for a year.

His commitment to God had compelled him to live a life of simplicity. He had pared down his possessions, giving his car to a homeless man. He dreamed of serving the poor in a third world country.

"God gives generously so we in turn can do the same," he told Rosy as he oiled the chain of his bike.

Rosy grew quiet.

His simple lifestyle seemed to contradict her fervent prayers for a thousand dollars. Was she wrong in asking God for so much?

"So what are your plans for the rest of the summer?" Lenny asked.

"I think...I'm...going to Israel," Rosy said.

She told him how she had always hoped to see the Holy Land.

"There's a trip scheduled for August. I can't afford it but I've been praying for a miracle," she said.

Lenny gave the tire on his bike a test twirl. "How much do you need?" he asked.

"A thousand dollars," she said.

Lenny smiled.

"You've been praying that God would answer a prayer of yours, and I've been praying that God would answer a prayer of mine."

He explained that he had recently inherited a large sum of money and that he'd been praying that God would show him what to do with it.

"But last week," he grinned, "I received an additional inheritance of a thousand dollars. Ever since, I've been asking God who it's for."

At first, Rosy didn't understand what he was saying.

"That person is you," Lenny said.

"Me?"

He nodded. "You!"

Minutes later, Lenny handed her a one thousand dollar check dated July 1.

"How should I repay you?" she asked.

Lenny wasn't at all concerned. "Pay it back to someone who needs it more than I do," he said.

So that August, Rosy went to Israel. She hiked along the rocks of the Jordan River, she swam in the cool aqua blue waters of the Mediterranean Sea, and she smelled the fragrant roses that framed the garden tomb of Jesus.

As she trod the homeland of God, she couldn't stop thinking about Lenny's generosity. By sharing an unconditional gift, Lenny had displayed the love of a gracious God who gives without measure or limits. It was a brand of giving that she would model for a lifetime.

Twenty years later, Rosy hasn't forgotten her commitment. Now a wife and mother, she spends her free time working with the poor, encouraging the lonely, and caring for the handicapped.

And whenever she hears of a financial need, she writes out a check, sending it off without a return address.

As she drops the anonymous gift in the mailbox, she remembers the words of Lenny, now a missionary to the poor of the third world. God gives generously so we can do the same.

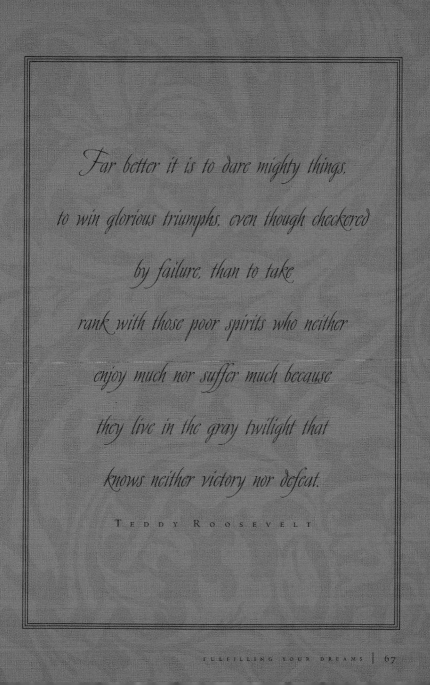

Far better it is to dare mighty things,

to win glorious triumphs, even though checkered

by failure, than to take

rank with those poor spirits who neither

enjoy much nor suffer much because

they live in the gray twilight that

knows neither victory nor defeat.

TEDDY ROOSEVELT

Choosing
Success

The true worth of a man
is to be measured
by the objects he pursues.

MARCUS AURELIUS

SANDCASTLES

by MAX LUCADO

from THE FINAL WEEK OF JESUS

*H*ot sun. Salty air. Rhythmic waves. A little boy is on the beach. On his knees he scoops and packs the sand with plastic shovels into a bright red bucket. Then he upends the bucket on the surface and lifts it. And, to the delight of the little architect, a castle tower is created.

All afternoon he will work. Spooning out the moat. Packing the walls. Bottle tops will be sentries. Popsicle sticks will be bridges. A sandcastle will be built.

Big city. Busy streets. Rumbling traffic.

A man is in his office. At his desk he shuffles papers into stacks and delegates assignments. He cradles the phone on his shoulder and punches the keyboard with his fingers. Numbers are juggled and contracts are signed and, much to the delight of the man, a profit is made.

All his life he will work. Formulating the plans. Forecasting the future. Annuities will be sentries. Capital gains will be bridges. An empire will be built.

Two builders of two castles. They have much in common. They shape granules into grandeurs. They see nothing and make something. They are diligent and determined. And for both the tide will rise and the end will come.

Yet that is where the similarities cease. For the boy sees the end while the man ignores it. Watch the boy as the dusk approaches.

As the waves near, the wise child jumps to his feet and begins to clap. There is no sorrow. No fear. No regret. He knew this would happen. He is not surprised. And when the great breaker crashes into his castle and his masterpiece is sucked into the sea, he smiles. He smiles, picks up his tools, takes his father's hand, and goes home.

The grown-up, however, is not so wise. As the wave of years collapses on his castle, he is terrified. He hovers over the sandy monument to protect it. He blocks the waves from the walls he has made. Saltwater soaked and shivering, he snarls at the incoming tide.

"It's my castle," he defies.

The ocean need not respond. Both know to whom the sand belongs....

I don't know much about sandcastles. But children do. Watch them and learn. Go ahead and build, but build with a child's heart. When the sun sets and the tides take—applaud. Salute the process of life, take your Father's hand, and go home.

Talent develops in quiet, alone;

character is sharpened in

the torrent of the world.

GOETHE

HOW SUCCESS WAS WON

by NANCY JO SULLIVAN

I aspired to be writer. And now here I was, sitting in the front row of my freshman English class, excited to be in college. I was an average student, or maybe even a little below average. Sitting in this classroom was the first hard-won step toward realizing my dream.

Then the instructor handed back the essays we had written a few days earlier. My heart sank as I saw the D+ that scarred the first page of my paper. I crumpled up my lofty aspirations along with the essay and stuffed it into my backpack, fighting back tears.

After class, I lingered at the professor's desk. I felt compelled to tell her that I wanted to be a writer. "Sister Mary, I'm not smart," I added.

She smiled at me kindly, her face framed by the deep charcoal gray of her nun's habit. "Hard work and divine grace...that's how success is won," she said.

She followed up this platitude later by inviting me to join her for breakfast after church the following Sunday. After eating waffles at a long pine table in her kitchen, she handed me a tablet and a silver pen and coached me into writing a good story. She showed me how to write first-class beginnings. She helped me with endings and with everything in between.

This continued Sunday after Sunday. Over bacon and eggs or muffins or toast, Sister cheered me on as I rewrote drafts and corrected punctuation.

"Dreams demand toil," she told me time and time again.

My grades climbed; I graduated. Now twenty years later, my written works have appeared in countless magazines. And to my delight, my first book, a collection of inspirational stories, was published last summer.

When I first took the book in my hands, I had to look twice to make sure it was really my name and not someone else's on the front cover. Awed, I paged through it and thought of Sister Mary. She had shown me that the path to achievement involved the willingness to develop one's God-given talents. In her eyes I had always been "smart." I had learned from her to claim my gifts and to "toil" toward my dreams. That's what success is all about.

Sister Mary, I thought, *you were so right.* I was holding the reward of her wisdom in my hands.

The Riddle

AUTHOR UNKNOWN

I am your constant companion.

I am your greatest helper or heaviest burden.

I will push you onward or drag you down to failure.

I am completely at your command.

Half the things you do might just as well be turned

over to me and I will be able to do them quickly and correctly.

I am easily managed—you must merely be firm with me.

Show me exactly how you want something done

and after a few lessons I will do it automatically.

I am the servant of all great people and, alas, of all failures, as well.

Those who are great, I have made great.

Those who are failures, I have made failures.

I am not a machine, though I work with all the precision

of a machine plus the intelligence of a person.

You may run me for profit or run me for ruin——

it makes no difference to me.

Take me, train me, be firm with me,

and I will place the world at your feet.

Be easy with me and I will destroy you.

Who am I?

I am habit!

"For I know the plans I have for you," declares the LORD, "plans
to prosper you and not to harm you, plans to give you hope and
a future. Then you will call upon me and come and pray to me,
and I will listen to you. You will seek me and find me when you
seek me with all your heart."

JEREMIAH 29:11–13

NEW INTERNATIONAL VERSION

Long-Range Vision

by Howard Hendricks

As a boy I loved to wander over to a nearby park and watch the older men play checkers. One day one of them invited me to play. At first it looked easy. I captured one, then another of his checkers. But then, suddenly, he took one checker and hopped and skipped right across the board to the border and yelled, "King me!" With that king, he proceeded to wipe me off the board.

That day I learned about long-range vision. No one minds losing a few checkers if he's headed for king territory.

IN THE SCHOOL OF DECISIONS

by JOE LO MUSIO

There is the story of the young executive who, in seeking advice from a gray-haired colleague, asked, "Can you tell me what has been the secret of your success?"

"The secret, friend, is two words: right decisions!" replied the older man.

"But how do you make right decisions?"

"One word," came the answer, "experience."

"But how do you get experience?"

The old man smiled. "Two words: wrong decisions!"

We will continue to learn

the rest of our lives.

We will learn from our failures

and our successes.

We will learn by growing older,

by suffering, by loving,

by taking risk, and by accepting

what we cannot change.

KATHLEEN BRADY

GRADUATION SPEECH

HEAD HUNTER

by JOSH McDOWELL

from BUILDING YOUR SELF-IMAGE

An executive hirer, a "head hunter" who goes out and hires corporation executives for other firms, once told me, "When I get an executive that I'm trying to hire for someone else, I like to disarm him. I offer him a drink, take my coat off, then my vest, undo my tie, throw up my feet and talk about baseball, football, family, whatever, until he's all relaxed. Then, when I think I've got him relaxed, I lean over, look him square in the eye and say, 'What's your purpose in life?' It's amazing how top executives fall apart at that question.

"Well, I was interviewing this fellow the other day, had him all disarmed, with my feet up on his desk, talking about football. Then I leaned up and said, 'What's your purpose in life, Bob?' And he said, without blinking an eye, 'To go to heaven and take as many people with me as I can.' For the first time in my career I was speechless."

Each person's work is a portrait of himself.

SAMUEL BUTLER

I Tried to Climb the Mountain Today

Mountain Today

by Gary Barnes

I tried to climb the mountain today.   As I inched my way up the path, I felt out of breath and I had to turn back.

I tried to climb the mountain today. But it was so hot outside, I thought I had better stay in my nice air-conditioned house and rest up for tomorrow's attempt.

I tried to climb the mountain today. On my journey, darkness started to fall and I was full of fear, so I had to return to a safe place.

I was ready to climb the mountain today. But I had so many other things to do, so instead of climbing the mountain I took care of much more important tasks. I washed my car, mowed the grass, and watched the big game. Today the mountain will just have to wait.

I was going to climb the mountain today. But as I stared at the mountain in its majestic beauty, I knew I stood no chance of making it to the top, so I figured why even bother trying.

I have forgotten about climbing the mountain today, until a friend came by and asked me what I was up to lately. I told him I was thinking about climbing that mountain some day. I went on and on about how I was going to accomplish this task.

Finally he said, "I just got back from climbing the mountain. For the longest time I told myself I was trying to climb the mountain but never made any progress.

"I almost let the dream of making it to the top die. I came up with every excuse of why I could not make it up the mountain, but never once did I give myself a reason why I could. One day as I stared at the mountain and pondered, I realized that if I didn't make an attempt at this dream all my dreams will eventually die.

"The next morning, I started my climb," he continued. "It was not easy, and at times I wanted to quit. But no matter what I faced, I placed one foot in front of the other, keeping a steady pace. When the wind tried to blow me over the edge, I kept walking. When the voices inside my head screamed, 'Stop!' I focused on my goal, never letting it out of sight, and I kept moving forward. At times, I was ready to quit, but I knew I had come too far. Time and time again, I reassured myself that I was going to finish this journey. I struggled to make it to the top, but I climbed the mountain!

"I have to be going," my friend said. "Tomorrow is a new day to accomplish more dreams. By the way, what are you going to do tomorrow?"

I looked at him, with intensity and confidence in my eyes, and said, "I have a mountain to climb."

The only thing we can be certain of in life is
change. Like the metamorphosis of a caterpillar to
a butterfly, we must pass from one state into
another, unfolding from what we are today into all
that we are capable of being.

SARAH VOGT

COMMENCEMENT SPEECH

TRAGEDY TO TRIUMPH

from GOD'S LITTLE LESSONS ON LIFE FOR GRADUATES

One winter night, a man was driving two young women to a meeting when they came upon a multiple-car collision. They were unable to stop on the slick road before they slammed into the back of a car. One of the girls, Donna, was thrown face-first through the windshield. The jagged edges of the broken windshield made horrible gashes in her face.

At the hospital, a plastic surgeon took great care in stitching Donna's face. Nevertheless, the driver dreaded visiting Donna. He expected to find her sad and depressed. Instead, he found her happy and bright, refusing to let the accident destroy her joy.

As Donna slowly recovered she became intrigued by the work of the doctors and nurses. She later studied and became a nurse, met a young doctor, married him, and then had two children. Years later she admitted that the accident was one of the best things that ever happened to her.

We are free to choose our attitude in every circumstance. We can choose to let trouble leave us depressed and weak, or we can choose to become happy and strong in spite of our trials. When we choose to have joy, our worst tragedies can be turned into our greatest triumphs.

There are two choices,

two paths to take.

One is easy and that

is its only reward.

AUTHOR UNKNOWN

Finding Inspiration

You will find, as you look back upon your life,

that the moments that stand out are the

moments when you have done things for others.

HENRY DRUMMOND

THE JUGGLER

by BILLY GRAHAM

retold by ALICE GRAY

*H*e was born in Italy but came to the United States as a young man. He studied juggling and became famous throughout the whole world.

Finally he decided to retire. He longed to return to his home country and settle down. He took all his worldly possessions, booked a passage on a ship to Italy, and invested all the rest of the money in a single diamond. He hid the diamond in his stateroom.

While aboard ship, he was showing a boy how he could juggle a bunch of apples. Soon a crowd had gathered. The pride of the moment went to his head. He ran to his stateroom and got the diamond. He explained to the crowd that it represented his entire life's savings. He started juggling the diamond. Soon he was taking more and more chances.

At one point he threw the diamond high into the air and the crowd gasped. Knowing what the diamond meant, they begged him not to do it again. Moved by the excitement of the moment, he threw the diamond even higher. Again the crowed gasped and then sighed in relief when he caught the diamond.

Having total confidence in himself and his ability, the juggler told the crowd he would throw it up one more time. This time it would be so high that it would be out of sight for a moment. Again, they begged him not to do it.

But with the confidence of all his years of experience, he threw the diamond high into the air. It actually did disappear for a moment. Then the diamond returned into view, sparkling in the sunlight. At that very moment, the ship lurched and the diamond dropped into the sea, lost forever.

We all feel terrible about the man's loss of all his worldly possessions. But God compares our soul as more valuable than the possessions of the whole world.

Just like the man in the story, some of us are juggling with our souls. We trust in ourselves and our own ability and the fact that we have gotten by before. Oftentimes there are people around us begging us to stop taking the risk because they recognize the value of our soul.

But we continue to juggle one more time. . .never knowing when the ship will lurch and we will have lost our chance forever.

"What will it profit a man

if he gains the whole world

and loses his own soul?"

MARK 8:36

NEW KING JAMES VERSION

My business is not to remake myself,

but to make the absolute best

of what God made.

ROBERT BROWNING

A New Way of Seeing

by KIMA JUDE

*C*risp autumn weather urged us into the outdoors. My three college roommates and I decided to take a break from studying to toss a Frisbee, sit in the grass, and watch people. As I waited in the car for my friends, I turned my face toward the sun and smiled.

Nearby, a man in an overcoat caught my eye. He had a full head of gray hair yet was clearly in robust health. Except for his vision.

He wore dark glasses and swept a white cane across the ground in front of him. He was walking in a peculiar pattern, his stride purposeful and at the same time somewhat aimless. It seemed that he had strayed from the sidewalk onto a dirt knoll covered with fallen leaves. The area was just broad enough that the full arc of his cane did not reach the sidewalk for which he was searching.

I watched as he moved from one end of the knoll to the other, walking in circles, getting nowhere. I couldn't see his eyes behind the dark glasses but his frustration was obvious. I marveled at the desire for independence that seemed to drive men like this, solitary and sightless, into the world.

Just then my friends returned, oblivious to the man a few yards from the car. As we drove away, I shared the poignant scene and how moved I was by his courage.

"But why didn't you help him?" one friend asked.

An obvious question, even at the time, and it startled me. *Why didn't I help him?* That question nagged at me for several days. What was missing in me that I was content to sit there and observe this man's struggle without even asking if I could help? Maybe I'd spent too much time in classes studying and taking notes. Maybe I'd become too much a student of life instead of a participant in it. I tried to convince myself that I was respecting a man's choice for independence. But the detached way I watched through glass was disquieting.

Some weeks later, while walking at a brisk pace to class, I passed a man out walking his dog. When I got to the corner I quickly scanned the road to make sure there was no traffic. When the *Walk* signal appeared, I stepped into the street.

Behind me, the dog barked. I glanced over my shoulder and stopped short, right in the middle of the intersection. The dog wore a harness—a trained seeing-eye dog—and he was straining to lead this blind man across the street. The young man, unsure of the traffic condition, tried to restrain his four-legged guide.

This time, I recognized the opportunity. I had learned something about compassion—wisdom to know when help was needed and when to stand back.

"It's okay," I called to the young man, waiting to see if he'd accept my help.

After a brief moment, the man gave his dog the lead and stepped out into the street. The dog calmed down and joyfully led his master ahead. Deliberately, I shortened my stride and allowed them to pass me.

We reached the other side; he went his way and I went mine. I took the time to help this young man without offending him or taking away his independence, and that felt good. I still made it to class on time, this time without lingering regret or nagging questions. Once in class I took notes and made observations about life, just as before—but this time I thought about how lessons are really learned. Some of the most important ones cannot be taught in a laboratory or by lecture. Instead, our wise and gentle God sends them into our very paths.

And when there is a lesson to learn, He gently pushes us again and again until we begin to understand. The lessons He sends always apply, often in ways we don't expect. Two strangers crossed my path and I began to learn sensitivity for the needs of other people—the need for help versus the need for independence. All along, God knew what lessons were needed.

You see, a short time later my younger sister lost most of her eyesight to diabetes. Fleeting disquiet once moved me to godly change, and that change now moves me to reach out with compassion in a very personal way.

It's Up to You

CATHERINE MANCEAUX

One song can spark a moment,
> One flower can wake the dream.

One tree can start a forest,
> One bird can herald spring.

One smile begins a friendship,
> One handclasp lifts a soul.

One star can guide a ship at sea,
> One word can frame the goal.

One vote can change a nation,
> One sunbeam lights a room.

One candle wipes out darkness,
> One laugh will conquer gloom.

One step must start each journey,
> One word must start each prayer.

One hope will raise our spirits,
> One touch can show you care.

One voice can speak with wisdom,
> One heart can know what's true.

One life can make the difference,
> You see, it's up to YOU!

*I don't have to have
a perfect plan for my life
because God does.*

MANDY STRAUSSER

GRADUATION SPEECH

THE FINAL I FAILED

by BERNICE BROOKS

from STUFF YOU DON'T HAVE TO PRAY ABOUT

Finals week had arrived with all its stress. I had been up late cramming for an exam. Now, as I slumped in my seat, I felt like a spring that had been wound too tight. I had two tests back-to-back, and I was anxious to get through with them. At the same time I expected to be able to maintain my straight-A grade point average.

As I waited impatiently for the professor to arrive, a stranger walked up to the blackboard and began to write:

Due to a conflict, your professor is unable to give you your test in this classroom. He is waiting for you in the gymnasium.

Oh, great, I thought. Now I have to walk clear across campus just to take this stupid exam.

The entire class was scurrying out the door and rushing to the gym. No one wanted to be late for the final, and we weren't wasting time talking.

The route to the gym took us past the hospital. There was a man stumbling around in front of it. I recognized him as the young blind man whose wife had just given birth to a baby in that hospital. He had been there before, but he must have become confused.

Oh, well, I told myself. Someone will come along soon and help him. I just don't have time to stop now.

So I hurried along with the rest of the class on our way to take that final exam.

As we continued down the sidewalk, a woman came rushing out of a nearby bookstore. She had a baby on one arm, a stack of books on the other, and a worried look on her face. The books fell onto the sidewalk, and the baby began to cry as she stooped to pick them up.

She should have left that kid at home, I thought. I dodged her as the class and I rushed along.

Just around the next corner someone had left a dog on a leash tied to a tree. He was a big, friendly mutt, and we had all seen him there before, but today he couldn't quite reach the pan of water left for him. He was straining at his leash and whining.

I thought, What cruel pet owner would tie up a dog and not leave his water where he could reach it? But I hurried on.

As we neared the gym, a car passed us and parked close to the door. I recognized the man who got out as one of the maintenance crew. I also noticed he left the lights on.

"He's going to have a problem when he tries to start that car to go home tonight," the fellow next to me said.

By that time we were going in the doors of the gym, the maintenance man waved a greeting to us and disappeared down one of the halls. We found seats close to where our teacher waited.

The professor stood with his arms folded, looking at us. We looked back. The silence became uncomfortable. We all knew his tests were also teaching tools, and we wondered what he was up to. He motioned toward the door, and in walked the blind man, the young mother with her baby, a girl holding the big dog on a leash, and the maintenance man.

These people had been planted along the way in an effort to test whether or not the class had grasped the meaning behind the story of the Good Samaritan and the man who fell among thieves. We all failed.

"Now which of these three would you say was a neighbor to the man who was attacked by bandits?" Jesus asked.

The man replied, "The one who showed him mercy."

LUKE 10:36–37
NEW LIVING TRANSLATION

Choosing Humility

H. DALE BURKE AND JAC LA TOUR

from A LOVE THAT NEVER FAILS

The humble can wait patiently,

while the arrogant wants it now!

The humble demonstrates kindness,

while the arrogant doesn't even notice the need.

The humble are content, not jealous or envious,

while the arrogant feel they deserve more.

The humble honors and esteems the other,

while the arrogant brags on himself.

The humble does not act unbecomingly,

while the arrogant's manners are rude.

The humble shows a servant spirit,

while the arrogant demands to be served.

The humble are not easily provoked,

while the arrogant are quick to take offense.

The humble quickly forgive a wrong suffered,

while the arrogant can't rest until they even the score.

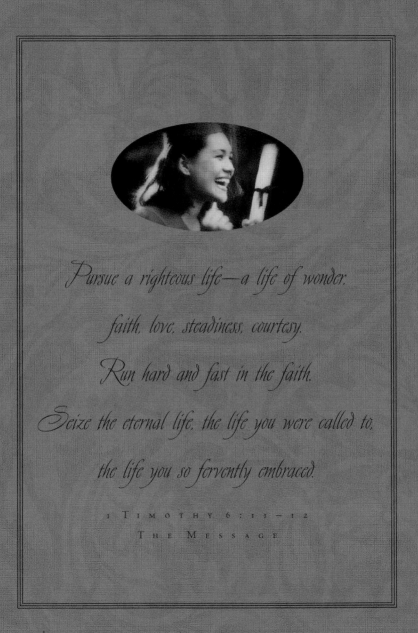

Pursue a righteous life—a life of wonder,

faith, love, steadiness, courtesy.

Run hard and fast in the faith.

Seize the eternal life, the life you were called to,

the life you so fervently embraced.

1 TIMOTHY 6:11–12
THE MESSAGE

A PRICELESS TREASURE

by SANDY CLOUGH

from SO RARE A TREASURE

*A*s I was cleaning my dorm room one day when I was in college, I came across a small Bible with a white leather cover on the bookshelf. It had been a gift to me from an aunt of a young man I had dated for quite some time. In our Southern culture, the inference was clear. It was to be carried with a wedding bouquet someday. But that Bible wasn't going to be used in that way because I had ended the relationship. I held the Bible up to my roommate. "What am I going to do with this?"

She looked at it and at me and wryly said, "Why don't you read it?"

Another Bible, a very old Bible with a lot of "character," appears in several of my paintings. It has thumb indexes, ragged pages, and a well-used appearance. I appreciate its usefulness to me, but I don't even remember where I got it. And, as you have probably guessed, I have never read it, either.

The Bible that is dear to me is not the one that is pretty or the one that is old; it is the one I have read and that I still read. It has been a treasure chest to me. When I opened it, I found real life and the very heart of God Himself. In fact, I like to think of the notes I've written and the verses I've underlined as a map to immeasurable treasure. This is treasure that is not hidden at all but just waiting to be found and possessed. In its pages I have found peace, wisdom, encouragement, hope, instruction, and love.

A Guy Named Bill

by Rebecca Manley Pippert

adapted from Out of the Saltshaker

His name is Bill. He has wild hair, wears T-shirts with holes in them, jeans, and no shoes. This was literally his wardrobe for his entire four years of college. He is brilliant. Kind of esoteric and very collegiate. He became a Christian while attending college.

Across the street from the campus is a well-dressed, very conservative church. They want to develop a ministry to the students, but are not sure how to go about it.

One day Bill decides to go there. He walks in with no shoes, jeans, his T-shirt, and wild hair. The service has already started and so Bill starts down the aisle looking for a seat. The church is completely packed and he can't find a seat. By now people are looking a bit uncomfortable, but no one says anything. Bill gets closer and closer and closer to the pulpit and when he realizes there are no seats, he just squats down right on the carpet. (Although perfectly acceptable behavior at a college fellowship, trust me, this had never happened in this church before!)

By now the people are really uptight, and the tension in the air is thick. About this time, the minister realizes that from way at the back of the church, a deacon is slowly making his way toward Bill. Now the deacon is in his eighties, has silver-gray hair, a three-piece suit, and a pocket watch. A godly man, very elegant, very dignified, very courtly. He walks with a cane, and as he starts walking toward this boy, everyone is saying to themselves, *You can't blame him for what he's going to do. How can you expect a man of his age and of his background to understand some college kid on the floor?*

It takes a long time for the man to reach the boy. The church is utterly silent except for the clicking of the man's cane. All eyes are focused on him. You can't even hear anyone breathing. The people are thinking, *The minister can't even preach the sermon until the deacon does what he has to do.* And now they see this elderly man drop his cane on the floor. With great difficulty he lowers himself and sits down next to Bill and worships with him so he won't be alone. Everyone chokes up with emotion.

When the minister gains control he says, "What I'm about to preach, you will never remember. What you have just seen, you will never forget."

College-Bound Blessings

LINDA SHEPHERD

FROM LOVE'S LITTLE RECIPES FOR LIFE

I have held you close. Now as you fly into

adulthood, bound to open books and discover new

worlds, I release you. But not without one final

prayer—prosper not only in your studies, but

prosper in knowing God more richly.

I will not be there to catch you when you fall. But

God will catch you when I can't. Depend on Him and

learn to trust Him. You are not alone. Knowing this,

my empty nest will not seem so lonely. My heart

will soar as I watch you take wing.

Acknowledgments

ACKNOWLEDGMENTS

A diligent search has been made to trace original ownership, and when necessary, permission to reprint has been obtained. If I have overlooked giving proper credit to anyone, please accept my apologies. If you will contact Multnomah Publishers, Inc., Post Office Box 1720, Sisters, Oregon 97759, correction will be made prior to additional printings. Please provide detailed information.

Acknowledgments are listed by story title in the order they appear in the book. For permission to reprint any of the stories, please request permission from the original source listed below. We appreciate the authors, publishers, and agents who granted permission for reprinting these stories.

ALWAYS REMEMBER

"Remembering" by Max Lucado. Taken from *The Inspirational Study Bible* by Max Lucado, © 1995, Word Publishing, Nashville, TN. Used by permission. All rights reserved.

CHEERING YOU ON

"Graduation Speech" by Tim Wildmon, retold by Alice Gray. This story first appeared in the El Cajon, California, *Christian Times*. Used by permission of *AFA Journal.*

"You Can Do It!" by Ricky Byrdsong, with Dave and Neta Jackson. Taken from *Coaching Your Kids in the Game of Life*, © 1999. Reprinted with permission from the August 2000 *Reader's Digest* and Bethany House Publishers.

Quote by Adam Bollen excerpted from his graduation speech, Mountlake Terrace High School, 1999. Used by permission of the author.

Adam can be reached by email at bollena@cc.wwu.edu.

"Keeper of the Spring" by Charles R. Swindoll. Taken from *Improving Your Serve* by Charles Swindoll, © 1981, Word Publishing, Nashville, TN. Used by permission. All rights reserved.

"The Best...Not the Worst" by Ted Engstrom. Used by permission of the author.

"I Wish for You" by James N. Watkins, © 1997. Used by permission of the author. Jim surprised his daughter, Faith, by having the juniors of her show choir sing this song to the seniors during their final concert. You can hear the song and read excerpts from his twelve books for young people at www.jameswatkins.com.

FULFILLING YOUR DREAMS

Quote by Sarah McGhehey excerpted from her graduation speech, Sonrise Christian School, 2000. Used by permission of the author.

"Sparky" by Earl Nightingale. Taken from *More of...The Best of Bits and Pieces.* Reprinted by permission of The Economics Press, Inc., Fairfield, NJ 07004. Ph: 800-526-2554, Fax: 973-227-9742, e-mail: info@epinc.com. Website: www.epinc.com.

"Catsup Soup" by Cynthia Hamond, S.F.O., © 1998. Used by permission of the author. Cynthia has been in several of the Chicken Soup for the Soul books, magazines, and one of her stories was made for TV. She enjoys speaking and school visits. You may reach her at P.O. Box 488, Monticello, MN 55362, or by e-mail at Candbh@aol.com.

"Live!" by Emily Campagna. Used by permission of the author. Quoted from her high school graduation speech, Mountain View High School, 1999.

"If the Dream Is Big Enough...the Facts Don't Count" by Cynthia Stewart-Copier, © 1999. Used by permission of the author. Cynthia Stewart-Copier is an international speaker and author. Cynthia knows firsthand how to dream big and has dedicated her life to empower others to stand up, step out, and reach their dreams. She can be reached at www.daretodreambig.com.

"Rosy's Miracle" by Nancy Jo Sullivan. Taken from *Moments of Grace* by Nancy Jo Sullivan, © 2000. Used by permission of Multnomah Publishers, Inc., Sisters, OR.

Choosing Success

"Sandcastles" by Max Lucado. Taken from *The Final Week of Jesus* by Max Lucado, © 1994. Used by permission of Multnomah Publishers, Inc., Sisters, OR.

"How Success Was Won" by Nancy Jo Sullivan, © 2000. Used by permission of the author.

"Long-Range Vision" by Howard Hendricks. Used by permission of the author.

"In the School of Decisions" by Joe LoMusio, © 1986. Used by permission of the author.

Quote by Kathleen Brady excerpted from her graduation speech, Hope International University, 2000. Used by permission of the author.

"Head Hunter" by Josh McDowell. Taken from *Building Your Self-Image* by Josh McDowell, © 1984 by Campus Crusade for Christ, Inc. Used by permission of Tyndale House Publishers, Inc. All rights reserved.

"I Tried to Climb the Mountain Today" by Gary Barnes, © 1999. Used by permission of the author. Gary Barnes is the creator of Self-Worth.Com and The Motivational Mailer. To learn more about Gary, Self-Worth.Com, and The Motivational Mailer, visit: www.self-worth.com.

Quote by Sarah Vogt excerpted from her graduation speech, Dansville, 1999. Used by permission of the author.

"Tragedy to Triumph." Taken from *God's Little Lessons on Life for Graduates*, compiled by the Honor Books staff, © 1999. Used by permission of Honor Books, Tulsa, OK.

FINDING INSPIRATION

"The Juggler" by Billy Graham, retold by Alice Gray from an illustration heard on a television broadcast of a Billy Graham crusade in the 1980s.

"A New Way of Seeing" by Kima Jude, © 2000. Used by permission of the author. Kima Jude is a freelance journalist and writer. Now married and a mother, she obtained her journalism degree from Marshall University.

"It's Up to You" by Catherine Manceaux. Used by permission of the author. Catherine can be reached at wolf130@hotmail.com.

Quote by Mandy Strausser excerpted from her graduation speech, Sonrise Christian School, 2000. Used by permission of the author.

"The Final I Failed" by Bernice Brooks. Taken from *Stuff You Don't Have to Pray About* by Susie Shellenberger, © 1995. Used by permission of Broadman and Holman Publishers, Nashville, TN.

"Choosing Humility" by H. Dale Burke and Jac La Tour. Taken from *A Love That Never Fails* by H. Dale Burke and Jac La Tour, © 1999. Used by permission of Moody Press, Chicago, IL.

"A Priceless Treasure" by Sandy Clough. Taken from *So Rare a Treasure*, © 2000 by Sandy Lyman Clough. Published by Harvest House Publishers,

Eugene, OR 97402. Used by permission.

Photo Credits

David Bailey Photography

Full page photos: pages 7, 11, 12, 17, 18, 22, 26, 43, 44, 48, 60, 69, 70, 74, 77, 82, 95, 96, 106, 115, 116

Oval photos: pages 15, 35, 47, 57, 73, 80, 90, 111

Gary Buss/FPG International LLC

Inset photo: page 17

Oval photos: pages 32, 93

Steve McAlister/Image Bank

Inset photo: page 69

Oval photos: pages 21, 112

Photodisc

Scroll photo: pages 1, 13, 19, 23, 29, 33, 37, 45, 49, 53, 61, 71, 75, 81, 83, 85, 87, 91, 97, 101, 107, 113, 117

Small cap photo: pages 2, 10, 16, 42, 68, 94, 120, 128

Inset photos: pages 11, 43

Large background cap photo: cover and pages 3, 5, 121

Oval photos: pages 40, 59, 100

Super Stock

Inset photos: cover and pages 3, 7, 95, 120

Oval photos: pages 36, 86